@RosenTeenTalk

DEPRESSION

Christine Honders

ROSEN
PUBLISHING

NEW YORK

Published in 2021 by The Rosen Publishing Group, Inc.
29 East 21st Street, New York, NY 10010

First Edition

Editor: Theresa Emminizer
Designer: Michael Flynn
Interior Layout: Rachel Rising

Photo Credits: Cover, pp. 1, 3, 5, 27, 45 Olimpik/Shutterstock.com; cover Cosmic_Design/Shutterstock.com; cover, pp. 1, 6,8, 10, 12, 14, 16, 18, 20, 22, 24, 26, 28, 30, 32, 36, 40, 42 Vitya_M/Shutterstock.com; pp. 3, 22 kali9/Shutterstock.com; pp. 3, 14 Brocreative/Shutterstock.com; pp. 3, 30 Monkey Business Images/Shutterstock.com; pp. 3, 35 SDI Productions/ E+/Getty Images; pp. 3, 39 Thomas Barwick/ DigitalVision/Getty Images; p. 6 seabreezesky/Shutterstock.com; p. 7 Patrick Foto/Shutterstock.com; p. 8 Bruce Ayres/ The Image Bank/Getty Images; p. 9 Jakkrit Orrasri/Shutterstock.com; p. 11 Casarsa/ E+/Getty Images; p. 12 P_Wei/ E+/Getty Images; p. 13 vitranc/ E+/Getty Images; p. 16 Prazis Images/Shutterstock.com; p. 17 polikhay/Shutterstock.com; p. 18 FatCamera/ E+/Getty Images; p. 19 Ronald Sumners/Shutterstock.com; p. 20 sdecoret/Shutterstock.com; p. 21 maxim ibragimov/Shutterstock.com; p. 23 Aila Images/Shutterstock.com; p. 25 FatCamera/E+/Getty Images; p. 26 Happy Together/Shutterstock.com; p. 28 studiovin/Shutterstock.com; p. 29 Hank Grebe/Getty Images; p. 31 Ljupco Smokovski/Shutterstock.com; p. 32 Aleksandra Gigowska/Shutterstock.com; p. 33 BigTunaOnline/Shutterstock.com; p. 36 Ashley Corbin-Teich/ Image Source/Getty Images; p. 37 Lisa F.Young/Shutterstock.com; p. 40 Jon Kopaloff/Stringer/Getty Images Entertainment/Getty Images; p. 41 David M. Benett/ WireImage/Getty Images; p. 41 Axelle/Bauer-Griffin/ FilmMagic/Getty Images; p. 42 Jamie Wilson/Shutterstock.com; p. 42 suns design/Shutterstock.com; p. 43 LEE SNIDER PHOTO IMAGES/Shutterstock.com.

Some of the images in this book illustrate individuals who are models. The depictions do not imply actual situations or events.

Library of Congress Cataloging-in-Publication Data

Names: Honders, Christine, author.
Title: Depression / Christine Honders.
Description: New York : Rosen Publishing, [2021] | Series: @Rosenteentalk | Includes index.
Identifiers: LCCN 2020001324 | ISBN 9781499468090 (paperback) | ISBN 9781499468106 (library binding)
Subjects: LCSH: Depression in adolescence--Juvenile literature.
Classification: LCC RJ506.D4 H66 2021 | DDC 616.85/2700835--dc23
LC record available at https://lccn.loc.gov/2020001324

Manufactured in the United States of America

CPSIA Compliance Information: Batch #BSR20. For further information contact Rosen Publishing, New York, New York at 1-800-237-9932.

Find us on

CONTENTS

Chapter 1

What Is Depression?

Sophia's alarm went off. It was time for school. But even after a good night's sleep, Sophia felt tired. She didn't want to get out of bed.

Sophia thought about seeing her best friend, Carly, during lunch. They always sat together. Carly would make her laugh with funny stories. She still didn't move. Lately, not even Carly could make her smile. It's Tuesday, art club, Sophia thought. She used to love going to art club after school with her friends. But she hadn't felt like going in weeks. Plus she thought her artwork was terrible anyway.

What's wrong with me? Why am I so sad all the time? Sophia got tears in her eyes and pulled the blankets over her head.

People with depression stop doing the things they used to love. Nothing seems fun anymore.

IDENTIFYING DEPRESSION

It's normal to feel sad once in a while. But depression isn't regular sadness. Depression is a mood **disorder**. It changes the way a person thinks and acts. They can't see the good things in life. They have no energy or drive to do things. Depression causes problems at school, home, and even with friends.

Depression is more than just feeling down in the dumps. Depression can last for weeks or even months.

When you're depressed, you feel hopeless. It feels like no one understands your sadness. But depression is very common in teens. In fact, one in five teenagers have depression.

Fact!

Depression can cause other health problems. Some people get stomachaches or headaches. Some can't eat or eat too much. Others can't sleep and some never want to get out of bed.

SIGNS OF DEPRESSION

- You're always angry or sad.
- You stop doing things you love.
- You feel bad about yourself.
- You cry over everything.
- You have trouble paying attention or remembering things.
- You've tried drugs or alcohol to feel better.
- You feel hopeless and alone.

NEGATIVE THINKING

Negative thoughts are thoughts about problems or worries. People with depression can't stop their negative thoughts. They think that their problems are too hard to solve. They believe things will never get better. Negative thinking makes people think things are worse than they really are.

Suicide is the second leading cause of death for teenagers. If you feel suicidal, find someone to talk to right away.

People with depression also have negative thoughts about themselves. They think they're worthless. They believe no one could ever love them. Negative thoughts can make people believe that the world would be better off without them.

Remember

Suicide is NEVER a good answer. There is always a way to fix a problem, even if you can't see it yet.

Having thoughts of suicide does not make you a bad person. Depression makes people think and do things they don't usually do.

Find Help

If negative feelings make you feel so bad you want to hurt yourself, get help right away. Call the National Suicide Prevention Lifeline at 1-800-273-TALK (8255), 24 hours a day, 7 days a week. All calls are confidential, or private.

What Happened to Nathan?

Nathan and I are best friends. Every day after school we go to my house. We do our homework. Then we hang out together until dinnertime. Nathan and I have always gotten along.

But today was different. When I started walking with Nathan after school, Nathan went a different way. When I asked where he was going, Nathan yelled at me and said it was none of my business.

I felt confused and hurt. Had I done something wrong? I thought about how Nathan had been acting lately. He was a lot quieter when we were together. He'd also stopped doing his homework after school. He'd told me he didn't care about his grades. I can't understand what's happening to my best friend.

People with depression sometimes push their friends away. They don't feel like anyone can help them.

INVISIBLE DISORDER

People with depression may not know they're depressed. Negative thinking makes them believe they're losers. If they get bad grades, they think they're stupid. They may feel like a failure, or a bad person.

Depression makes people act differently. Someone who was once kind and friendly may suddenly act rude and mean.

Other people may not realize someone has depression. They may just think the person is lazy. They may also think they have a bad **attitude**. Depression makes them angry and difficult to get along with. This causes other people to keep their distance.

Chapter 2

CAUSES OF DEPRESSION

Depression sometimes runs in families. But not everyone with a depressed family member gets depression. Problems at home and school can cause depression. Major life changes can also cause depression, like breaking up with a boyfriend or girlfriend or losing a loved one.

The stress of being bullied can cause depression. Bullying is abuse and you don't have to take it. Tell an adult you can trust.

There are different kinds of depression. Some women get depressed after having a baby. Others get depressed during the winter months. People with **bipolar disorder** have major mood swings. They have times when they're depressed. And they have times when they're full of energy and excitement.

RISK FACTORS FOR DEPRESSION

- Serious illness or **disability**
- Alcohol or drug **abuse**
- Bullying
- Family problems
- Violence or abuse at home
- Loneliness
- Major life changes (death, divorce, or something else major)
- Dealing with sexual or gender identity
- Too much time on social media

LGBTQ Teens and Depression

- **Transgender** teens are four times as likely as other teens to have depression.
- Twenty-eight percent of LGBTQ youth said they felt depressed most or all of the time in the past month.

DEPRESSION IN LGBTQ TEENS

LGBTQ teens are at high risk for depression. Many feel they can't be themselves. They're made to feel ashamed for who they are. They're more likely to be bullied. They're also more likely to be threatened with violence.

Gay-straight **alliance** clubs help LGBTQ teens feel safe and welcomed at school.

Find Help

The It Gets Better Project (https://itgetsbetter.org/) connects LGBTQ youth around the world. It's a place for them to share their stories. They also have support for LGBTQ teens with problems like depression.

In 2015, it was reported that:

10% of LGBTQ teens were threatened or injured with a weapon at school.

34% were bullied at school.

28% were bullied through texts and social media.

LGBTQ students were 140% more likely to skip school at least once a month because they were scared someone might hurt them.

Being LGBTQ affects how someone thinks about themselves. Many people in the world are **prejudiced** against them. Terrible, untrue things are said about the LGBTQ community. Hearing these things all the time can make some LGBTQ teens feel unloved and hopeless.

ALCOHOL AND DRUGS

People with depression often drink and do drugs to make the sadness go away. Being high or drunk might make them feel better for a little while. But using drugs and alcohol over a long time makes depression worse.

There are **counselors** who help people with both depression and substance abuse. There are also support groups where they can talk to other people with the same problems.

Some people are more at risk for depression than others. They may have a parent with depression. They may have violence or abuse in their life. Abusing drugs or alcohol could also bring on an **episode** of depression.

Find Help

How Are Depression and Substance Abuse the Same?

- A part of our brain controls how we handle stress. That part is damaged, or harmed, by both depression and substance abuse.

- Substance abuse can also run in the family.

- Both can be treated.

DEPRESSION AND ABUSE

Kids who are abused are likely to have depression. Abuse can be physical or sexual. It can also be verbal, like when someone angrily **criticizes** or insults someone else. Some kids are neglected by their parents. This means no one pays attention to them.

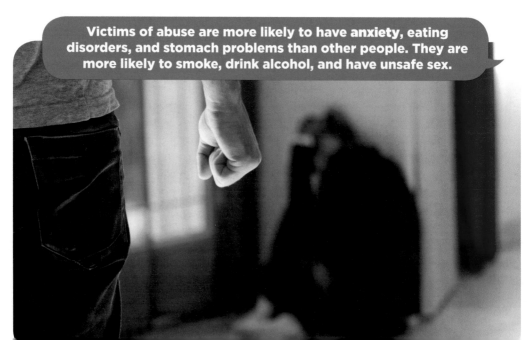

Victims of abuse are more likely to have **anxiety**, eating disorders, and stomach problems than other people. They are more likely to smoke, drink alcohol, and have unsafe sex.

Abuse makes kids feel hopeless. They feel they have no one to protect them. They think they aren't good enough for their parents. These feelings can cause low self-esteem. Having low self-esteem means you don't like yourself. This leads to depression.

Find Help

If you're being abused, call the National Domestic Violence Hotline at 1-800-787-3224.

STUDYING TRAUMA

Trauma is the experience of an event that is emotionally painful. In 1998, researchers created a study that grouped common childhood trauma experiences into 10 categories. It's known as the ACE study. The ACE study links childhood trauma to health risks, such as depression.

Chapter 3

TREATING DEPRESSION

People with depression may feel ashamed. They may feel bad about themselves because they can't just cheer up. But depression isn't something to be embarrassed about. Depression is one of the most common mental disorders in the United States.

Sometimes it helps to talk to a trusted adult. Letting them know you feel depressed is a good way to start working toward getting better.

Treating depression may be easier than you think. It can get better with medical care and therapy. If you think you have depression, you should see a doctor. The doctor will check to see if you have a physical illness. Some illnesses can make a person feel depressed.

Sicknesses That Look Like Depression

Hypothyroidism: the thyroid gland doesn't make enough **hormones**. It makes people feel tired and depressed.

Mono: a sickness that makes you feel exhausted all the time. It's hard to get through your daily activities.

Care

Depression is treated with medication, therapy, or both. Every person with depression is different. There isn't just one way to treat it. It may take some time to figure out the treatment that works best for you.

Tanisha's First Appointment

I was nervous. I was in the waiting room of a therapist's office. I'd never been to a therapist before. But lately I was feeling so sad and tired. I was crying a lot. My mom took me to my doctor, who said that I might have depression. The doctor said that therapy might help.

The therapist called my name. She was a pretty woman with a nice smile. I sat down in the office. The therapist said, "My name is Terry. What would you like to talk about?" I took a deep breath. I started telling Terry about myself. I told her about how hard 10th grade is and how sad I feel every day. As I talked, I thought, "Wow. I feel better already."

It's hard to talk about your feelings, especially when you're depressed. But opening up about them will make you feel less alone.

TALK THERAPY

Talk therapy helps figure out what your problems are. Then you talk about the problems and work on fixing them. Talk therapy can be one-on-one with a **licensed** therapist. Group therapy can also help people with depression. They're able to share problems with other people with depression. They help each other heal.

Online therapists are helpful for people who aren't comfortable going to an office.

Cognitive behavioral therapy (CBT) is very helpful in treating depression. It helps you understand negative thinking and how to change it. You learn to look at the world in a more positive way.

MEDICATION

Antidepressants are medicines that treat depression. They help your brain deal with your mood or stress. The medication can take up to six weeks to work. You should not stop taking it unless a doctor tells you. You also shouldn't drink alcohol or take drugs with the medication. Otherwise, it may not work.

Antidepressants can cause side effects. Some people get headaches or stomachaches. Others get too sleepy. You should tell your doctor if you have side effects.

Fact!

Some side effects of antidepressants are rare but very serious. Some teens say antidepressants make them feel more depressed, even suicidal. If someone is having these side effects, they should see a doctor right away.

This diagram shows that seeing a therapist is much more helpful than just taking medication. It also shows how many teens aren't being treated for depression. Teens may be embarrassed to admit they have depression. But not talking about it only makes it worse.

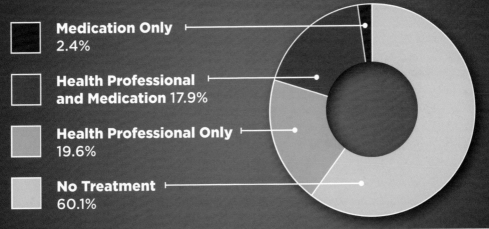

Treatments for Teens with Depression

- **Medication Only** 2.4%
- **Health Professional and Medication** 17.9%
- **Health Professional Only** 19.6%
- **No Treatment** 60.1%

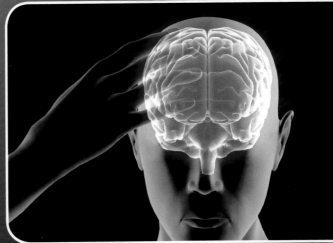

The depressed brain has much less activity than the healthy brain. Antidepressants can change the chemicals in the brain.

Chapter 4

SEE SOMETHING, SAY SOMETHING

You may have a friend who suddenly seems down. They tell you they feel stupid and worthless. They may stop hanging out with you. They've started to try drugs or alcohol. Your friend could have depression.

Depression can make your best friend seem like a stranger. Once they get help, they'll be back to the person they used to be.

Some teens don't like talking to adults. You may be the only person they're comfortable with. There are things you can do to help. Talk to them about why they're sad. Be a good listener. Encourage them to get help from an adult.

Act Now

If your friend talks about suicide, tell a trusted adult right away. Even if you promised your friend you wouldn't tell, tell anyway. They need your help. It's better to have an angry friend than one is who is no longer alive.

How Can I Help?

Listen, even if you don't understand why your friend is sad. Just knowing you're there is helpful to them.

Invite your friend to hang out with you.

Remind them that treatment will make them feel better.

Millions of people are on social media. Most posts are about happy things. But sometimes people talk about things not going well. They may post images that show that they're sad or lonely. What do you do if you see someone on social media threatening to hurt themselves?

If you see a post about someone threatening suicide, take it seriously. Call 911 immediately. If you know the person, call the National Suicide Prevention Lifeline for advice. You can also use the Crisis Text Line ("4HOPE" to 741-741).

Find Help

If you see someone threatening self-harm on YouTube, you can flag the video. Click on the three dots in the bottom right corner. Select "Report" and then "Harmful dangerous acts." YouTube staff look at flagged videos every hour. They also work with suicide prevention groups to get help.

Reporting Suicidal Posts

Facebook Help Center
www.facebook.com/help/594991777257121/

Instagram Support
https://help.instagram.com

Snapchat Support
https://support.snapchat.com

Twitter: About Self-Harm and Suicide
https://help.twitter.com/en/safety-and-security
/self-harm-and-suicide

...ports through
...ial media sites
...y not get
...rd right away.
...u should still
...911 if you
...someone
...sting suicidal
...ssages.

Chapter 5

The Power of Healing

I was at my group therapy session. I had been **diagnosed** with depression a year ago. Group therapy and medication were helping me get better. There were new members in the group today. The therapist asked if anyone wanted to share their story. I raised my hand.

I told them about my depression. I talked about how my grades were so bad I stopped going to school. I told them that I started drinking every day. I talked about how angry I was at my parents for making me get help.

I told them that group therapy made me realize that I wasn't alone. I said, "Getting treatment was the best thing that ever happened to me. I'm just mad I didn't get it sooner."

Many people with depression blame themselves. Talking to others with depression makes them understand that depression isn't their fault.

SELF-CARE

There are things you can do to help yourself with depression. Accepting your feelings is the first step. It's also important to understand that depression doesn't make you a bad person.

Yoga is an exercise that helps with depression and stress. It teaches you to clear your mind using deep breathing and exercise.

It might be hard, but you should try to get out and do things. Spend time with people who make you feel good. Do an activity you used to love. **Volunteer** to do something nice for the community. You'll feel good about making someone else's life better.

Habits

Social media can make people feel more alone. They spend less time with real friends. Social media can also make you feel bad about yourself. Looking at other people's photos may make some people think everyone else is better looking or richer than they are. Taking a break from social media can help with depression.

Tools That Fight Depression

- Spend time outside.
- Take a long hot bath.
- Listen to music.
- List what you like about yourself.
- Read a good book.
- Play with a pet.
- Watch a funny movie.

Chapter 6

Healthy Habits

Healthy habits help with depression. Exercising gives your brain an instant rush! Even walking helps you feel better. You should also eat healthy foods. Stay away from junk food and sugary soda.

Teenagers need about eight hours of sleep every night. Sleeping too much or too little affects your mood. Getting more exercise will help you get a good night's sleep.

Stay away from drugs and alcohol. They might make you feel good now. But drugs and alcohol make depression worse in the long run.

Exercising causes a flood of chemicals to go into the brain. The chemicals make you feel instantly happy.

FAMOUS SUCCESS STORIES

Dwayne Johnson is one of Hollywood's most famous actors. He's also suffered from depression. As a teenager, his family was very poor. When he was 15, he stopped his mother from committing suicide. He failed out of college during his first year.

Dwayne Johnson says that many men and boys have a harder time admitting they have depression. He reminds them they're not alone.

Johnson says that he was depressed. He didn't want to go anywhere or do anything. But he picked himself back up. Johnson says that the key to fighting depression was opening up and talking about it.

Lady Gaga

Lady Gaga is another celebrity who isn't afraid to talk about her depression. Her Born This Way Foundation helps people with depression and other disorders. Her program teen Mental Health First Aid (tMHFA) teaches high school kids how to support each other.

J. K. Rowling

J. K. Rowling is the bestselling author of the Harry Potter books. While she wrote her first book, she was depressed. She said she used her negative thoughts to create evil characters. The characters fed off human happiness.

MORE RESOURCES

There are many places to get help if you have depression. Project Safe Place (1-888-290-7233) helps teens in crisis in 32 states. OK2TALK.org is an online community. Teens share stories, poems, music, and art about their depression.

Every 40 seconds, someone dies by suicide. World Mental Health Day helps people learn the signs of depression and how to prevent suicide.

The Jed Foundation helps schools start programs that support students with depression. Their website, SeizetheAwkward.org, is a good place to learn about mental illness. There are tips on how to talk to someone about depression. They also have positive stories from people who have beaten it.

Find Help

The Trevor Project is the only 24-hour suicide hotline for LGBTQ teens (1-866-U-TREVOR). TheTrevorProject.org gives LGBTQ teens a safe space online to ask questions. They also offer a free instant messaging service for immediate help.

More You Can Do

Learn about depression. Know what to do if someone you know is depressed.

Tell your friends and family that it's ok to talk about it!

Find out when Mental Health Awareness Day is. Help organize an event at your school.

Sophia's New Day

My alarm went off. I smiled. It was Tuesday, art club day. I couldn't wait to see my friends. I had some new paintings to show them. A text went off on my phone. It was Carly. I was going to see her at lunchtime.

I got ready for school. First, I took my antidepressant. About a month ago, I had gone to the doctor. I told her about how sad I was. The doctor said I might be depressed. I started taking medication every day. I also began talking to a therapist every week.

I feel like myself again. I know it won't always be easy. But this time I have the tools to cope with depression. I can live a happy, healthy life.

With treatment, most people with depression live a normal life.

GLOSSARY

abuse: To treat or use something in a wrong or unfair way; also, the act of doing so.

alliance: A close association formed between people or groups of people to reach a common goal.

anxiety: Fear about what might happen.

attitude: A feeling or way of thinking about something.

bipolar disorder: An illness that causes extreme mood changes.

cognitive: Of or relating to brain activities.

counselor: Someone who talks with people about their feelings and problems and who gives advice.

criticize: To find fault with something.

diagnose: To identify a disease by its signs and symptoms.

disability: A physical, mental, or developmental condition that limits a person's ability to do certain things.

disorder: A sickness or medical condition.

episode: An event.

hormones: Something that lives in body fluids and has an effect on the body.

licensed: Having a document required to practice a business, job, or activity.

negative: Not positive or helpful.

prejudice: An unfair feeling of dislike for a person or group because of race or religious or political beliefs.

suicide: The act of killing oneself.

transgender: A person whose gender identity is different from the sex they were identified with at birth.

volunteer: To do something to help because you want to do it.

INDEX